Map My Continent

by Jennifer Boothroyd

first step nonfiction

D1214436

Lerner Publications Company · Minneapolis

Copyright © 2014 by Lerner Publishing Group, Inc.

Main body text set in ITC Avant Garde Gothic Std Medium 21/25.
Typeface provided by Adobe Systems.

Lerner Publications Company
A division of Lerner Publishing Group, Inc.
241 First Avenue North
Minneapolis, MN 55401 U.S.A.

Website address: www.lernerbooks.com

Library of Congress Cataloging-in-Publication Data

Boothroyd, Jennifer, 1972–
    Map my continent / by Jennifer Boothroyd.
        p.   cm. — (First step nonfiction—Map it out)
    Includes index.
    ISBN 978–1–4677–1114–2 (lib. bdg. : alk. paper)
    ISBN 978–1–4677–1737–3 (eBook)
    1. Maps—Juvenile literature. I. Title.
GA105.6.B63 2014
526—dc23   2012045591

Manufactured in the United States of America
1 – PP – 7/15/13

Table of Contents

A Map 4

Planning a Map 9

Drawing a Map 14

How to Make a Continent Map 20

Fun Facts 22

Glossary 23

Index 24

A Map

We live in North America.
It is a **continent**.

I will make a **map** of my continent.

It will show the **location** of different places.

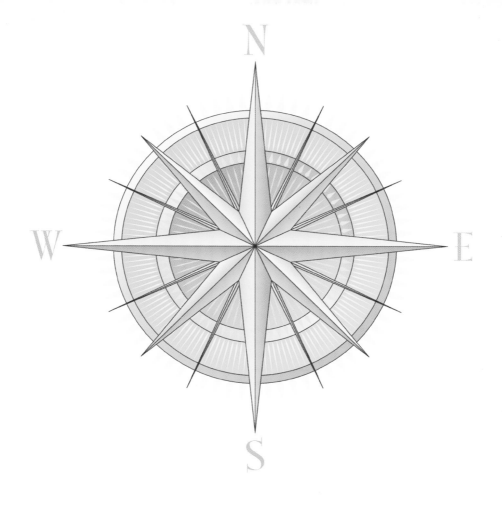

I will put a **compass rose** on my map.

It will show the four
directions. They are north,
south, east, and west.

Planning a Map

Countries	Mountains	Rivers	Lakes	Deserts
Belize	Chirripó Grande	Mackenzie	Great Bear Lake	Chihuahuan Desert
Canada	Gunnbjørn Fjeld	Mississippi	Lake Superior	Mojave Desert
Costa Rica	Mount McKinley	Rio Grande		
El Salvador	Mount Rainier			
Greenland	Mount Waddington			
Guatemala	Nevado de Toluca			
Honduras				
Mexico				
Nicaragua				
Panama				
United States				

This is a list of places for my map.

An **atlas** will help me find the places.

A map has **symbols**. They stand for places.

I will make blue lines like
this one for rivers.

I will make tan shapes like this one for deserts.

Drawing a Map

I have a blank map of the continent.

United States

Greenland

Canada

United States

Mexico

Belize
Honduras
Guatemala
Nicaragua
El Salvador
Costa Rica
Panama

I label the countries.

I label all the other places
I want on my map.

I draw a symbol for each place.

I add my compass rose.

I add a **key**. It tells what each symbol means.

How to Make a Continent Map

1. Ask an adult to print out a blank map of your continent.
2. Use an atlas or the Internet to learn where places are located on your continent.
3. Label each place that you want on your map.
4. Draw a symbol for each place.
5. Add a compass rose.
6. Add a key.

Fun Facts

- Earth has seven continents: Africa, Antarctica, Asia, Australia, Europe, North America, and South America.

- Asia is the world's largest continent. Australia is the smallest.

- Greenland is the world's largest island. It is part of North America.

- Asia has the most people. Antarctica has the least.

Glossary

atlas – a book of maps

compass rose – a symbol that shows directions on a map

continent – one of seven large land areas on Earth

key – the part of a map that explains the symbols

location – where something is

map – a drawing that shows where places are

symbols – things that stand for something else

Index

atlas – 10

compass rose – 7, 18

continent – 4–5, 14

countries – 15

deserts – 13

map – 5, 7, 9, 11, 14, 16

rivers – 12

symbols – 11, 17, 19